PROPERTY OF THE STATE OF ILLINOIS
SCHOOL YEAR _____ 95 '96 _____

SCHO   ICT 103
LIBRARY-MEDIA CENTER
4100 JOLIET AVENUE
LYONS, IL. 60534

M000248852

Rocks, Rocks
Big & Small

For Arvid, Vicky, and Jim—J.B.
For my parents, Bill and Billie Augsburger—H.P.

Produced by Daniel Weiss Associates, Inc.
33 West 17 Street, New York, NY 10011

Text copyright © 1990 Daniel Weiss Associates, Inc.,
and Al Jarnow

Illustration copyright © 1990 Heidi Petach

FIRST FACTS™ is a trademark of Daniel Weiss Associates, Inc.
All rights reserved. No part of this book may be used
or reproduced in any manner whatsoever without written
permission from the publisher.

Published by Silver Press, a division of
Silver Burdett Press, Inc., Simon & Schuster, Inc.
Prentice Hall Bldg., Englewood Cliffs, NJ 07632
For information address: Silver Press.

Printed in the United States of America
10 9 8 7 6 5 4

Library of Congress Cataloging-in-Publication Data

Barkan, Joanne.
Rocks, Rocks Big and Small / written by Joanne Barkan; illustrated
by Heidi Petach.
p.   cm.—(First facts)
Summary: An introduction to rocks, their origins, and their evolution.
1. Rocks—Juvenile literature.   [1. Rocks.]   I. Petach, Heidi,
ill.   II. Title.   III. Series: First facts
(Englewood Cliffs, N.J.)
QE432.2.B37 1989   89-39192
552—dc20   CIP
                                                AC
ISBN 0-671-68660-7   ISBN 0-671-68656-9 (lib. bdg.)

First Facts™

Rocks, Rocks Big & Small

Written by Joanne Barkan
Illustrated by Heidi Petach

Silver Press

Gigantic or tiny.
Rough or smooth.
Dull or shiny.
Red, yellow, green, or blue.
What are they?

Rocks!

The Earth is made of rock.
That's why you can find pieces of rock
in so many places: in the park,
in the woods, on the beach,
along canyons and cliffs,
and in your own backyard.

Sometimes you'll even find
a small rock in your shoe. Ouch!

Look at the rock called granite
under a magnifying glass.
You'll see it's made of gray,
pink, white, and black grains.
These grains are minerals.

Some rocks, such as granite,
are made of several minerals.
Some rocks, such as quartz,
are made of just one mineral.

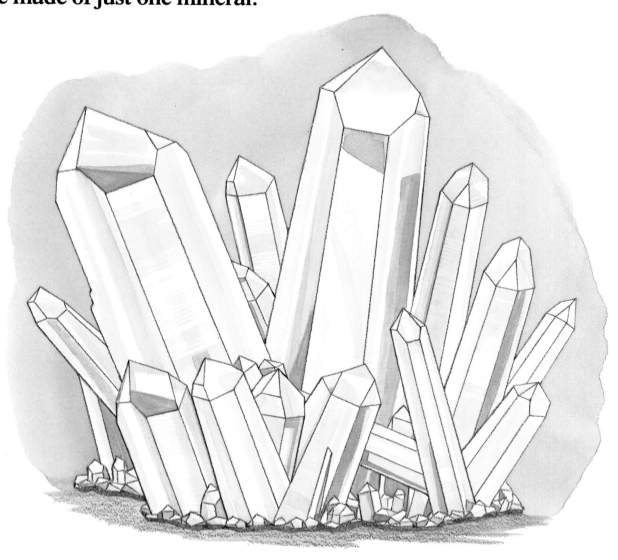

Where do the rocks you see come from?
Some rocks come from deep inside the Earth
where it's very hot—
so hot that the rock melts!

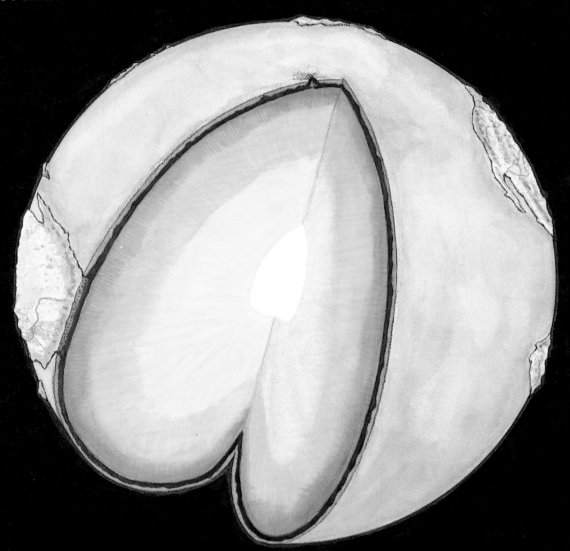

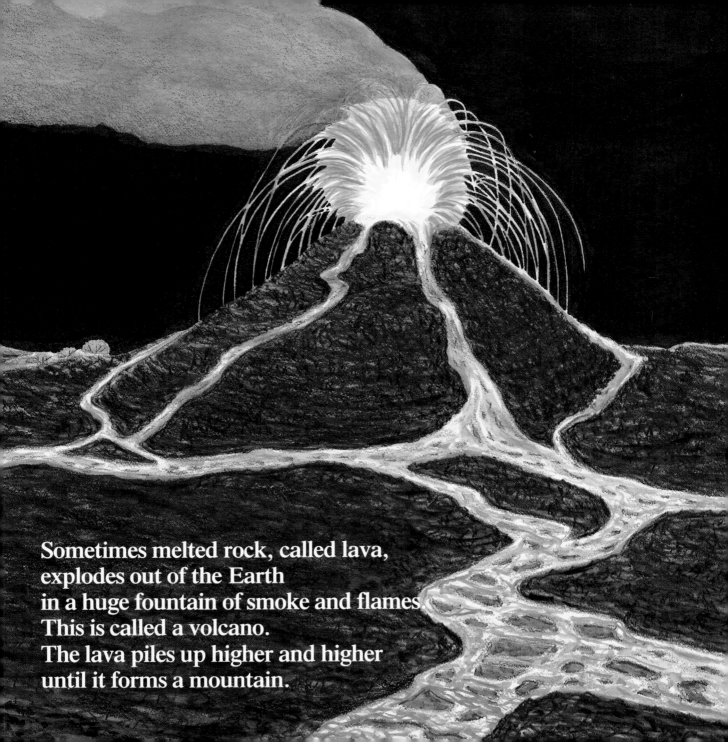

Sometimes melted rock, called lava,
explodes out of the Earth
in a huge fountain of smoke and flames.
This is called a volcano.
The lava piles up higher and higher
until it forms a mountain.

When melted rock from a volcano cools,
it becomes hard rock.
Many rocks you see today came from volcanoes
thousands or even millions of years ago.

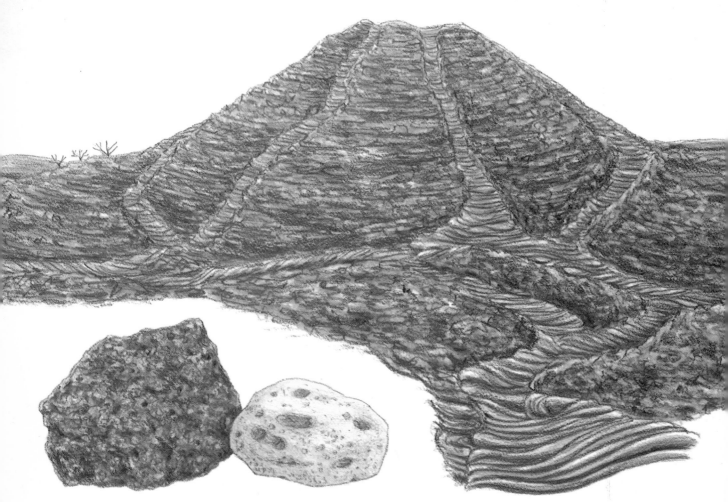

Rocks called basalt and pumice come from volcanoes.

Pumice can float in water
because it has many tiny airholes.

Sometimes layers of broken rock
are pressed together so hard
that they form new rocks.
Limestone and shale are made this way.

Heat and even more pressing can change a rock again.

Limestone can turn into pretty marble.

Shale can turn into smooth slate.

Rocks *never* stop changing.
Rain beats down on them.
Snow and ice bury them.
Wind drives sand and pebbles
against them.

Rivers swirl them along
for hundreds of miles.
Oceans toss them around and around
and then throw them onto the beaches.
All this wears down rocks
or breaks them into small pieces.

Some rocks are so worn down that
you'd never guess they were rocks.
Bury your feet deep in the sand at the beach.
Each grain of sand is a tiny bit of rock.

Shape a lump of clay into a ball or a boat.
Clay is made from worn-down rocks.

Dig a hole in the soil in your backyard.
Soil is made of tiny bits of rock and dead plants.

Some rocks contain the shells or skeletons of animals that have been dead for millions of years. Some rocks contain plants that are just as old. All these rocks are called fossils.

Scientists study fossils to find out
what the Earth was like long ago.
The next time you see a wall or a floor
made out of limestone, look at it carefully.
You might discover an animal shell!

You can find rocks in every color of the rainbow.
Many years ago, people ground up rocks
to get colored powders called pigments.
They used the pigments to make paints and dyes.

Azurite made a deep blue.

Malachite made a rich green.

Cinnabar made a brilliant red.

Pigments can still be made this way.
But scientists have found easier and safer
ways to make them in laboratories.

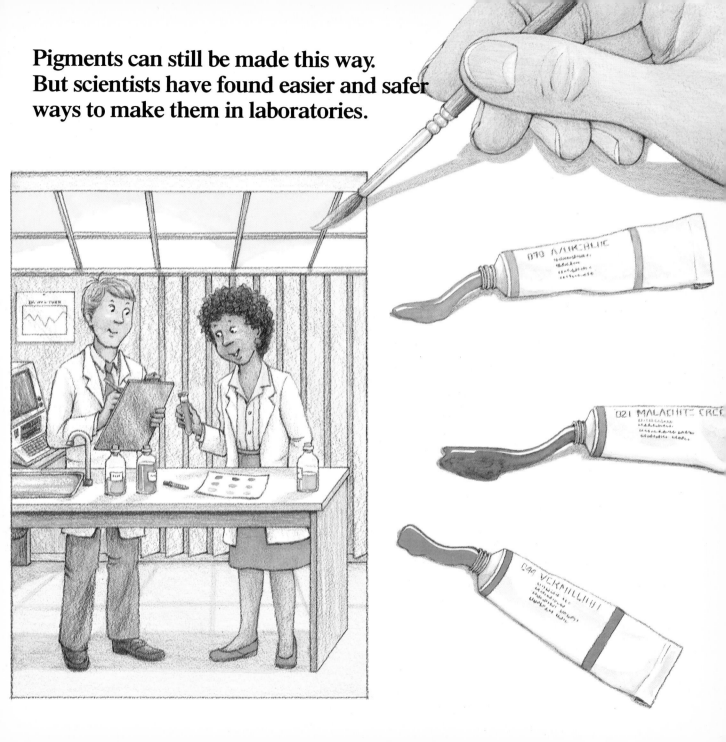

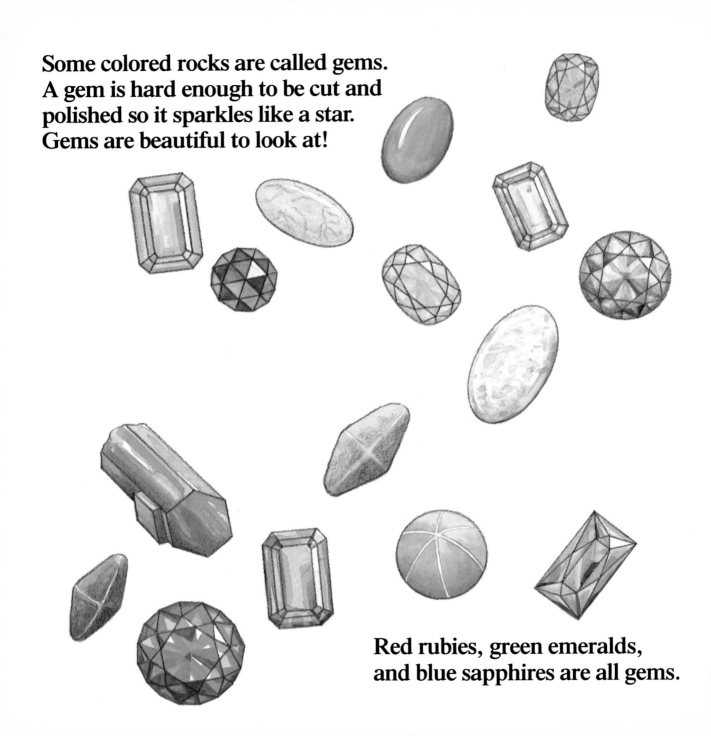

Some colored rocks are called gems.
A gem is hard enough to be cut and
polished so it sparkles like a star.
Gems are beautiful to look at!

Red rubies, green emeralds,
and blue sapphires are all gems.

Most diamonds have no color, yet they are
one of the most precious gems of all.
Diamonds are also the hardest kind of rock.
Only a diamond can cut another diamond!

People have always used rocks.
Thousands of years ago, rocks were used as tools.

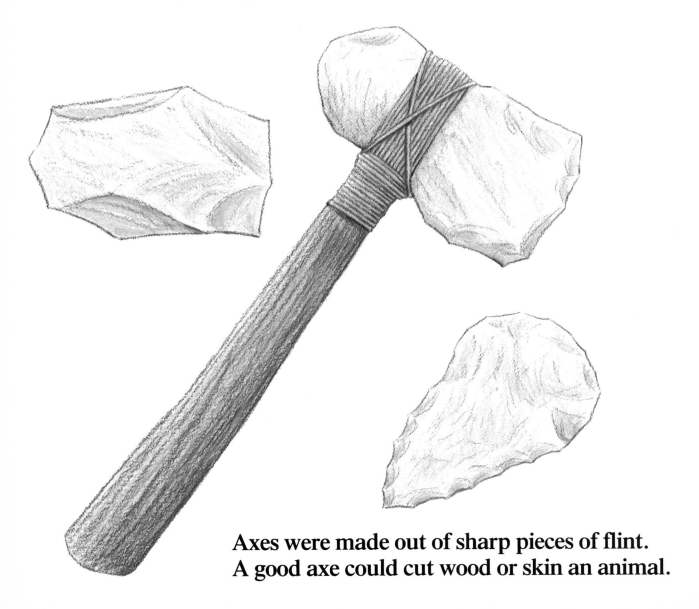

Axes were made out of sharp pieces of flint.
A good axe could cut wood or skin an animal.

Hammers were made by tying rocks to strong sticks.

Arrowheads were made by chipping a piece of
flint until it had a sharp point.

We still use rocks in many ways.
We crush limestone to make cement sidewalks.

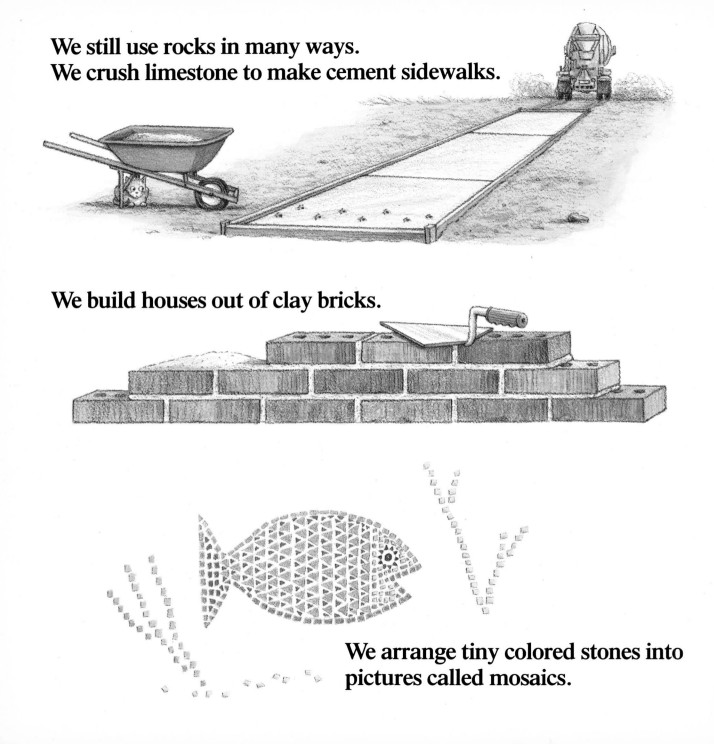

We build houses out of clay bricks.

We arrange tiny colored stones into pictures called mosaics.

Sculptors carve statues out of marble.
They can cut marble into any shape they want.
Then they can polish it
to bring out the beautiful colors.

Do you know what a rock hound is?
A rock hound is a person who always
looks for interesting rocks to collect.
You can be a rock hound, too.
Wherever you go, keep your eyes open
for strange and pretty rocks.

You might find them near a lake, in the woods,
or right in front of your house.
You can trade rocks with a friend.
Here's a smooth blue one for that shiny pink!

Some of the rocks you find
will be tiny and plain.
But just think of how long they've traveled
and all the places they've been.
If rocks could talk,
wouldn't they have wonderful stories to tell?